Emmanuel Crespel

Travels in North America

Emmanuel Crespel

Travels in North America

ISBN/EAN: 9783742875167

Manufactured in Europe, USA, Canada, Australia, Japa

Cover: Foto ©Andreas Hilbeck / pixelio.de

Manufactured and distributed by brebook publishing software (www.brebook.com)

Emmanuel Crespel

Travels in North America

TRAVELS

IN

NORTH AMERICA,

BY M. CRESPEL.

WITH A

NARRATIVE OF HIS SHIPWRECK,

AND EXTRAORDINARY

HARDSHIPS AND SUFFERINGS

ON THE

ISLAND OF ANTICOSTI;

AND AN

ACCOUNT OF THAT ISLAND,

AND OF THE

SHIPWRECK

OF HIS

MAJESTY's SHIP ACTIVE,

AND OTHERS.

London:

PRINTED BY AND FOR
SAMPSON LOW, BERWICK STREET, SOHO.

1797.

INTRODUCTION.

SOME apology may be thought necessary for introducing to the Public the following Narrative of a transaction which happened at so distant a period of time; but a recent event, the Shipwreck of Lord Dorchester on the Island of Anticosti, suggested an idea that the Public would be glad to receive an account of a spot on the globe hitherto little known, even by name, except to those navigators who sail up the river of St. Lawrence.

The Island of Anticosti has been long dreaded for shipwrecks; as long **ago** as the year 1690, when **Sir** William Phipps was returning down the river from his unsuccessful attack on **Quebec, a brig** of the fleet, with **sixty men on** board, being separated from the rest, struck on this island, and the people on board had only time to land their provisions before the **ship sunk.** The captain and his men, finding they must inevitably winter on the island, built a storehouse and nine small huts, from the planks of the wreck, to shelter them from the cold; but their provisions were so short, that they agreed

agreed that each man's allowance per week fhould be no more than two bifcuits, half a pound of pork, half a pound of flour, one pint and a quarter of peafe, and two falt fifh. It was not long before the difmal effects of hunger and cold began to appear among them, for on the 20th of December their doctor died, and after him thirty or forty more in a few weeks; and though they were all convinced of the neceffity of keeping to their allowance, unlefs they would at laft eat one another, yet their ftorehoufe was frequently broke open: an Irifhman once got to the provifions, and eat no lefs than eighteen

eighteen biscuits, which swelled him to such a degree, that he was forced to have his belly stroked, and bathed before the fire, to prevent its bursting. On the 25th of March five of the company resolved to venture out to sea in their skiff, which they lengthened out so far as to make a sort of cabin for two or three men, and having got a small sail, they shipped their share of provisions on board, and steered away for Boston; it was the 9th of May before these poor wretches arrived there, through a thousand dangers, from the sea and the ice, and almost quite starved with hunger and cold:

cold: upon their arrival, a veſſel was immediately difpatched away to the iſland, which in a few weeks brought off their friends who were left behind.

Soon after the conqueſt of Canada, an Engliſh ſhip, bound out to Quebec very late in the feaſon, had likewiſe the misfortune to be loſt on this defert iſland; her crew and paſſengers wintered there; endured inexpreſſible hardſhips from cold and hunger, and were indebted for their prefervation principally to a cargo of French wine which they had on board, a large quantity of which afforded

afforded them sufficient nourishment to sustain life, when almost every other species of sustenance failed. The translator has exerted himself to procure a narrative of their sufferings; but this, from the deaths of the persons who were on board, and no such narrative being preserved in print, he was unable to accomplish.

The captain and crew of his Majesty's ship Active, on board of which Lord Dorchester and his family embarked last year, were much more fortunate; they were shipwrecked at a more early period of the season, and preserved their boat,

boat, which being fitted up and sent to Halifax, a king's ship was difpatched, and brought the whole of the paffengers and crew away in fafety.

The following affecting narrative was publifhed in France, and written, in the form of a letter, from M. Crefpel to his brother; and, befides an account of his fufferings by fhipwreck, contains a previous detail of his travels in Canada, and in fome parts of that province but little known, and at that time but poorly inhabited.

M. Cref-

M. Crefpel feems a man of a religious turn of mind, fometimes bordering on enthufiafm; and perhaps fome of the readers would have been as well pleafed if part, or all of his reflections had been omitted; but as they all arife naturally from his fubject, and fhew a zeal which, in the temper of his mind, was highly worthy of praife, it was judged beft not to omit them.

The following defcription of the ifland of Anticofti was drawn up by Mr. T. WRIGHT, who wintered there, and furveyed the ifland by order of government.

The

The Ifland of Anticofti is fituated at the entrance of the river St. Lawrence, between the parallels of 49 deg. 4 min. and 49 deg. 53 min. 15 fec. N. latitude, and the meridians of 61 deg. 58 min. and 64 deg. 35 min. Weft longitude from London, determined by ten obfervations on the eclipfes of Jupiter's firft Satellite. Its circumference is 282 ftatute miles, its length 129 miles, and its breadth from 32 to 12 miles. This ifland contains 1,699,840 acres of very indifferent land; the nature of the foil and natural produce as follows:

(xiv)

The land in general is composed of a light-coloured stone, which is of a soft crumbling nature, and in some parts is mixed with clay. After digging to the depth of about two feet, you meet with small flat stones, with scarce any other mixture.

The sea coast, from the South-West point, to the West point, (including Ellis Bay and Observation River), is in height from 20 to 50 feet, and is mostly covered with woods to the water's edge.

Ellis Bay affords the only shelter for vessels in this large island, and that but a very indifferent one, which would be greatly exposed to the southerly winds, were it not for the shoals which extend from each side of the entrance, near two thirds of the distance across the bay, by which means they retard the violence of the sea; but at the same time, they endanger vessels in entering the bay with a wind on shore, by causing a great swell on the bar, on which there is but $2\frac{1}{2}$ fathoms water.

The land at the bottom of this bay is low marsh, and produces small birch, and spruce trees of different sorts.

Observation River is the largest, and runs the greatest distance of any in the island. We measured eight leagues up it without determining its length. This river is remarkable; for, notwithstanding its steep banks, which in the middle of the island are rocky bluffs about 100 feet in height, it is fordable almost in every part, except where it empties itself into the sea. The bottom is

stony,

stony, and the water exceeding clear. This river will admit of small vessels at the entrance, and at the time of high water, which is very regular here at the full and change of the moon, at $2\frac{1}{2}$ hours.

The entrance of it is formed by two gravel points, which are continually shifting their situation in a gale of wind from the westward, so that at one time its breadth will not be more than 20 yards, and at other times 150 yards, and in the fall of the year is liable to be entirely choaked up, so as to be impassable, which

really

really happened when the equinoctial gales prevailed in the month of September, a few days after we had got our vessel into the river.

I am of opinion, that the seal fishery might be carried on here with some success in the spring of the year; these creatures, at the time of high water, enter the river in great bodies, and are very careful to be out again before the tide quits them, which might be easily prevented by a net properly placed at the entrance of the river.

The

The Sea-cows frequent the South-West point in the fall of the year, but not many in number, and in such a place as would render it impossible to cut them off.

This island is so well watered, that in the space of every mile round its coast you will either meet with a small rivulet or run of fresh water.

The land, from the South-West point to the East point, is chiefly low heaths of black turf, such as is used for fuel; bears no wood for the space of one to two miles

from

from the sea shore, and contains many small lakes and ponds, where a prodigious number of wild fowl resort in the spring to breed up their young.

The land on the North side, from the West point to Bear Cape, is very hilly near the middle of the island, and well wooded with birch, spruce, and pine of a middling size, the largest not exceeding fifteen inches diameter.

These hills, with a gradual descent, form an edging of low grass land with willow trees along the sea coast.

The

The island, from Bear Cape to the East point, contains several small bays, the extreme points of which are high white cliffs, which lose themselves in a regular descent, and form between them a fine low sand beach, out of which issues several rivulets or streams of fresh water.

The fruits, herbs, plants, and vegetables, which are the natural produce of this island, are cranberries, gooseberries, strawberries, huckleberries, red Indian-berries, juniper-berries, peas, parsley, onions, lambsquaters, or wild spinnage,

nage, Indian potatoes, sarsaparilla, maiden-hair, and Indian tea.

The Bears, who are the principal inhabitants of this island, are so numerous, that in the space of six weeks we killed fifty-three, and might have destroyed twice that number if we had thought fit. These animals, during the winter season, live in the hollows under the roots of trees, and it is asserted for fact, that they receive no other kind of nourishment during that time but from sucking their paws. It is indeed highly probable, that they live in a torpid a torpid state in severe frosts, as we neither saw one of them, or even their tracts in the snow during the winter. They come out of their holes in the month of April, exceedingly poor, and feed on fish and sea weed that is cast on shore. In the summer, they feed on berries and roots, for which they search very diligently, by grubbing along the sea shore after the manner of swine. These animals have been so little molested by mankind, that we have frequently passed near them without their discovering the least fear; nor did they ever shew any

incli-

inclination to attack us, except only the females in defence of their young. The largeſt of theſe bears weigh about 300 pounds, and are very good meat.

In this iſland there are alſo foxes, martins, and otters; the foxes are very numerous, and are of two colours, the ſilver gray and red; partridges are ſcarce, and are entirely white.

Of the water fowl there are the greateſt plenty, and ſome of them of a ſpecies peculiar to this country.

Fiſh

Fish are very scarce along the coast of this island, except near the east point, where, about the distance of three leagues to the northward of that point, is a small fishing bank.

Whales (that have been wounded, and escaped) are sometimes cast on shore on the south side of this island; for the south-west point forming a long bay with the west point, and facing the westward, a prevailing wind from that quarter, and a strong current setting down the river St. Lawrence, drives them ashore on this part of the island, where the Indians

dians from the main land, crossing over in the summer to hunt, frequently find them.

The winter that we spent on this island was very severe, there being frost at different times, from the 15th day of September, to the 21st day of June following, on which day I broke a thin skin of ice on a pond, and on the 31st day of May measured a bank of snow which lay near the sea, eleven feet perpendicular height, and half a mile in length. We had two continued frosts night and day, the one lasted from the 14th day of November to the 6th day

day of January, and the other from the 12th of the fame month to the 23d day of March following; during each of thefe fet frofts the thermometer was from ten, twenty, thirty, to forty-feven degrees below the freezing mark, and the fea feldom to be feen for the quantity of ice and fnow which was fpread over its furface.

There is a report which prevails amongft the French, but how well grounded I cannot fay, that a filver mine was difcovered on the fouth fide of this ifland, up a fmall river about fix leagues from the weft point, and that fome of the

the ore was taken to France, but I had not time to make a proper search **after it**.

A great number of vessels have formerly been wrecked on the eastern part of this island, which may now easily be accounted for, as by the best draughts hitherto made it appears on the present actual sur**vey, to** be twelve leagues short of **its real** length, and considerably **out of** its situation both in latitude and longitude.

VOYAGE,

VOYAGE, TRAVELS,

&c. &c.

You may remember that, towards the end of the year 1723, I received permission of my superiors to embark for the New World, a favour I had long solicited. I therefore proceeded to Paris, and received a licence from father Guisdron, Provincial of St. Denis, who had the direction of the missions in New France, or Canada.

Proceeding from thence to Rochelle, and having there procured every thing necessary for my passage, I **embarked in the** ship Camel, sailed on the 24th of May, 1724, and arrived at Quebec after a passage of ten weeks.

Here I remained till the year 1726; **and here M. de** la Croix, the Bishop of Quebec, conferred the priesthood upon me, and soon after appointed me curate of a village called Forel, situated to the south of of the river St. Lawrence, between the towns of Three-Rivers and Montreal.

Quebec, the capital of the province of Canada, or New France, is singularly situated, being a hundred and twenty leagues from the sea, and yet possessing a harbour capable of containing a hundred sail of line of battle ships. The river St. Lawrence is here about a mile broad, although below it is from four to five leagues. The first thing which strikes you on your arrival, is a fine falling sheet of water, called the Falls of Montmorenci, which is about

about thirty feet in breadth, and forty in height.

The city, which stands between the rivers St. Lawrence and St. Charles, consists of two towns. In the lower town, the merchants and **traders live**; and the passage from thence to the upper town is so steep, that it has been found necessary to cut steps, and therefore can only be ascended on foot. In the upper town are the cathedral, the seminary, and place of arms. The fortifications are not complete, but they have been long employed in rendering it a place of strength. It was, however,

however, sufficiently strong to resist the attacks of the English in 1711. The number of inhabitants are reckoned at seven thousand, many of whom are worth money, and exert themselves to make life as agreeable and cheerful as they can. Both sexes here have as fine complexions as any people in the world; are gay and sprightly; and although situated in a colony at such a distance from Europe, and locked up, by the severity of their climate, from the rest of the world for more than half the year, are extremely polite and engaging in their manners.

Three-

Three-Rivers is a town called so from its situation, which contains about **seven or ei**ght hundred inhabitants, and is one of the most ancient towns in the colony, and owed its rise to the great resort of Indians from the most distant **quarters,** by means of its three rivers. This port, next to Montreal, is the most important for trade in all Canada. There is plenty of iron found **in** its neighbourhood, and they **are** now beginning to work the mines. The Jesuits made a settlement, a few leagues below this place, with all the Indian converts they could collect; but, by a series of war and diseases, it was soon destroyed.

Two years after I was drawn from my curacy to go Chaplain to a party of four hundred French, which the Marquis de Beauharnois commanded, and who were to be joined by eight or nine hundred Indians of several nations, particularly Iroquois, who inhabit the south of the river St. Lawrence, between the English and French colonies*, by the Hurons and Nipissings,

* M. Crespel does not say what induced the French Government of Canada to undertake this expedition; and it cannot

B 4   escape

(8)

sings, and the Outawahs, who lived on the lakes and rivers of those names. To these, M. Peset, a priest, and Father Bertonniere, a Jesuit, acted as Chaplains. The whole, under the command of M. de Lignerie, were dispatched with orders to *destroy* a nation of Indians, called, by the French, the Fox Indians, but, in their own language, the Outagamies, situated on lake Michigan, about four hundred and fifty leagues from Montreal.

escape observation, that this *Christian* priest talks of destroying a whole nation of innocent Indians with great coolness and composure.

The

The Iroquois Indians inhabit the south side of the river St. Lawrence, between the English and French colonies, and are the most powerful, warlike, and politic people among the natives of North America. They consist of six confederate nations, and their form of government somewhat resembles that of the Swiss Cantons. Many of these Iroquois are settled in the interior of the French colony in villages, are converted, and as submissive to the French government as Indians can be made. They have rendered us good services, particularly in war time.

The Hurons are situated between lakes Huron, Eri, and Ontario. The Nipissings, to the north east of lake Huron.

We set off the 5th of June, 1728, and ascended the great river which bears the name of the Outawahs, and is full of falls and carrying places. We quitted it at Matawan, to enter a river which leads into lake Nipissing; the length of this river is about thirty leagues, and, like that of the Outawahs, full of falls and carrying places. From this river we entered the lake, whose breadth is about eight leagues; after crossing which, the river of the French carried

carried us quickly into lake Huron, into which it falls, after having run a courſe of thirty leagues with great rapidity.

As it was not poſſible ſo many perſons could go down theſe ſmall rivers together, it was agreed, that thoſe who paſſed down firſt, ſhould wait for the others at the entrance of lake Huron, in a place called La Prairie, which is a very fine ſituation. Here, for the firſt time, I ſaw a rattle-ſnake, whoſe bite is ſaid to be mortal, but none of us received any injury.

The

The 26th of July we were all assembled together, and I celebrated mass, which I had hitherto deferred; next day we departed for Michilimakinac, a post situated between the lakes Huron and Michigan. Although the distance was one hundred leagues, we ran it in less than six days. Here we remained some time to repair what had been damaged in the falls and carrying places; and here I consecrated two pair of colours, and interred two soldiers, who were carried off by fatigue and illness.

Michilimakinac is a post advantageously situated for trade, with three great lakes—Michigan, which is three hundred leagues in circuit; Huron, which is full three hundred and fifty leagues in circumference; and lake Superior, which is full five hundred leagues round: all three navigable for the largeſt ſort of boats, and the two firſt ſeparated only by a ſmall ſtrait, which has water ſufficient for ſmall veſſels, who can ſail, without any obſtacle over lake Eri, to the poſt of Niagara.

The 10th of Auguſt we left Machilimakinac, and entered lake Michigan. As we had contrary winds for two days, our Indians had time

to

to hunt, and they brought in two elks and a *caribou*, and were generous enough to offer us a part. We made some difficulties in receiving their favour, but they forced us, and told us, that since we had shared with them the fatigues of the journey, it was but just we should partake of the comforts it had procured, and that they should not esteem themselves men if they did not act thus to their brethren. This answer, which was spoken in French, affected me sensibly. What humanity among those we call savages! and how many should we find in Europe to whom that title might be more properly applied!

The

The generosity of our Indians deserved a lively sense of gratitude from us. Several times, when we had not been able to find places for hunting, we had been obliged to live on salt meat. The flesh of the elks and *caribou* removed the distaste we began to entertain for our ordinary food.

The *Orignal*, or Elk of Canada, is as large as a horse, and his horns as long as those of a stag, but thicker, and more inclining over the back, the tail short, and his skin a mixture of light gray and reddish black. The Caribou is not so tall, and
shaped

shaped more like the afs, but equals the ftag in fwiftnefs.

The **14th of** the fame month **we** continued our route as far as the ftrait of Chicagou, and paffing from thence to Cape La Mort, which is five leagues, we encountered a gale of wind that drove feveral of our canoes on fhore who could not double the cape and fhelter themfelves under it: feveral **were** loft, **and the** men diftributed among **the** other canoes, who by great good **fortune** efcaped the danger.

The

The 15th we landed among the Malomines, with a view to provoke them to oppose our descent; they fell into the snare, and were entirely defeated.

These Indians are called by the French *Folles Avoines*, or Wild-Oat Indians, probably from their living chiefly on that sort of grain. The whole nation consists only of this village, who are some of the tallest and handsomest men in Canada.

The next day we encamped at the entrance of a river named La Gasparde; our Indians entered

tered the woods, and brought back several deer, a kind of game very common in this place, and which supplied us with provisions for some days.

We halted on the 17th from noon to evening, to avoid arriving at the post of La Baye before night, wishing to surprise our enemies, whom we knew to be in company with the Saguis, our allies, whose village lay near **Fort St. Francis.** We advanced in the evening, and at midnight reached our fort at the entrance of the Fox river. As soon as we arrived, Monsieur de Lignerie sent some Frenchmen to

the

the commandant to know for certain if there were any enemies in the village, and being affured there were, he fent all the Indians, and a a detachment of the French, acrofs the river Le Sur, round the habitations, while the reft of the French entered by the direct way. However we had endeavoured to conceal our arrival, the enemies had information, and all the inhabitants efcaped except four, who were delivered to our Indians; and they, after having long amufed themfelves with tormenting them, fhot them with arrows.

I was

I was a painful witness of this cruel transaction, and could not reconcile the brutal pleasure they took in tormenting these unfortunate people, and making them suffer the pain of twenty deaths before they deprived them of life, with the generous sentiments expressed by these same savages a few days ago. I wished to have asked them, if they did not perceive the striking contrast in their conduct, and to point out what I thought reprehensible in their proceeding; but as all our interpreters were on the other side of the river, I was obliged to postpone my inquiries till another time.

After

After this affair we ascended the Fox river, which is much troubled with rapids, and whose course is near forty leagues. The 24th of August we arrived at the village of the *Puans* Indians, whose name, in their language, does not bear the same signification as in French, but from their vicinity to the waters, and they may therefore be more properly called the Maritime Indians. Our people were well disposed to destroy such men as they should find there, but the flight of **the** inhabitants saved them, and we **could** only burn their huts, and destroy the harvest of Indian corn, on which they subsist.

We

We afterwards croffed the little lake of the Foxes, and encamped at the **end**. The next day being St. Lawrence, we had mafs*, and entered a fmall river which led us to a marfhy ground, on the borders of which **was** fituated the chief fettlement of thofe Indians of whom we were in fearch. Their allies, the Saguis, had given them notice of our approach; they did not think proper to wait our arrival, and we found in their village fome women only, whom our Indians made flaves, and an old man, whom they

---

* How eafy does this pious miffionary pafs from havock and deftruction to devotion.

burned

burned by a flow fire, without manifesting the least repugnance for committing so barbarous an action.

This cruelty appeared to me more atrocious than that they had exercised on the four Saguis. I seized this opportunity to satisfy my curiosity on the subject I before-mentioned. Among our Frenchmen we had one who spoke the Iroquois language, whom I desired to tell the Indians, that I was surprised to see them, with so much apparent pleasure, inflict such a cruel death on an unfortunate old man; that the laws of war did not extend so far, and that it appeared to me, that such barbarity

barbarity gave the lie to all those good principles they pretended to entertain towards mankind. One of the Iroquois answered, that if any of them should fall into the hands of the Foxes or Saguis, they would experience still more cruel treatment, and that it was a custom with them to treat their enemies as they should be treated by them if they were taken.

I wished much to have been acquainted with the language of this Indian, to have shewn him what was blameable in his answer; but was obliged to content myself with desiring my interpreter to represent to him, that nature and religion still more required that we should be humane towards one another, and that moderation should guide us in all our actions; that pardon, and a forgiveness of injuries, was a virtue, the practice of which was expressly commanded by heaven; that I conceived it would not be safe for them to spare the Fox or Saguis Indians, but that if they put them to death, it should be as foes to their nation, and not as their private enemies; that such revenge was criminal, and that to exercise such excesses as they **had** towards the five unfortunate men they had put to death with such cruel torments, in some degree justified

juſtified the barbarity with which they reproached their enemies; that the **laws of war** only permitted **them to** take the life of their enemy, and not to glut themſelves with his blood, or drive them to deſpair by deſtroying them in any other way **than by combat** and arms: in fine, that they ought to ſet the Foxes and Saguis that example of moderation which is the proof of a good heart, and which makes the Chriſtian Religion, **and** thoſe who profeſs it, ſo much loved and admired.

I do not know whether my interpreter explained my ſentiments clearly, but the Indian could not be brought

brought to confefs that he acted on a falfe principle. I was proceeding to urge further reafons, when orders were given to advance againft the laft poft of the enemy, which was fituated on a little river which runs into another river that communicates with the Miffiffippi.

We did not find any Indians, and as we had no orders to advance further, we employed fome days in laying wafte the country, to deprive the enemy of the means of fubfiftence. The country hereabout is beautiful, the land fertile, the game plenty and good, the nights were
very

very cold, but the days extremely hot.

After this expedition, if such a useless march deserves that **name**, we prepared to return to Montreal, from **which we** were now four hundred and fifty leagues distant. In our passage we destroyed the fort at La Baye, because being so near **the enemy** it would not afford a **secure** retreat to the French, who must be left as a garrison. The Fox Indians, irritated by our ravages, and convinced that we should scarcely make a second visit into a country where we were uncertain of meeting with any inhabitants, might

have

have blockaded the fort, and perhaps have taken it. When we arrived at Michilimakinac, our commander gave permission to every one to go where he pleased. We had now three hundred leagues to travel, and our provisions would have fallen short if we had not exerted ourselves to make a quick passage. The winds favoured us in crossing lake Huron; but we had continual rains while we were on the river of the French, while crossing lake Michigan, and on the river Matawan, which ceased as we entered the river of the Outawahs. I cannot describe the swiftness with which we descended this great river, of which

imagi-

imagination only can form an idea. As I was in **a canoe** with some men whom experience had taught how to descend the rapids, I was not one of the last at Montreal, where I arrived the 28th of September, and remained **there till** the spring, when I received orders to proceed to Quebec.

Montreal, the second city in Canada, is of a quadrangular form, situated on the bank of a river, which gently rising divides the city into the upper and lower town. In the lower is an hospital, magazines, and place of arms; and in the upper, the seminary, church, convent of

the

the Recollêts, and governor's house. Montreal is situated on a fine island, about ten leagues in length, and four leagues in its greatest breadth, formed by two branches of the river St. Lawrence.

I no sooner reached that city than our commissary ordered me for Niagara, then a new settlement, with a fortress situated at the entrance of a fine river of the same name, formed by the celebrated cataract of Niagara, which lies south of lake Ontario, and six leagues from our fort.

I therefore returned to Montreal, and passed from thence to fort Frontiniac,

tiniac, or Cataraquoy, built at the entrance of lake Ontario. Although only **eighty** leagues from Montreal, as we went againſt the ſtream of the river, we were fifteen days in aſcending. Here we quitted our canoe, and embarked in a veſſel of **the** king's, built for the navigation of the lake, of about eighty tons burden, very ſwift, and which ſometimes croſſes the lake, a paſſage **of ſeventy** leagues, in thirty-ſix hours. The lake is very ſafe, being deep, and without rocks; I ſounded in the middle with an hundred fathom of line, and could find no bottom. It is about thirty leagues broad, and ninety long.

We

We failed the **22d** of July, but did not arrive until the 25th. I found the place very agreeable; hunting and fishing were very productive, the woods in their greatest beauty, and full of walnut and chesnut trees, oaks, elms, and some others, far superior to any we see in France.

The fever soon destroyed the pleasures we began to find, and much incommoded us until the beginning of autumn, which season dispelled the unwholesome air. We passed the winter very quietly, and would have passed it very agreeably, if the vessel which was to have brought us us refreshments had not encountered a storm on the lake, and been obliged to **put back** to Frontiniac, which **laid** us under the necessity of drinking nothing but water. As the winter advanced, she dared not to proceed, and we did not receive our stores **till May.**

In the spring I made a journey to Detroit, on the invitation of a brother **of our order,** who was there **on a mission.** From Niagara to this post is an hundred leagues, which is situated about fifteen leagues on this side the extremity of lake Erie.

This

This lake is about a hundred leagues long, and thirty broad, is shallow, and consequently dangerous in stormy weather. To the northward it is troubled with shoals, so that if a vessel is taken by the wind in a place where there is no good landing, which sometimes is not to be found in a space of three leagues, there is great danger of perishing.

In seventeen days I reached Detroit, and was received by the priest I went to visit with a warmth which shewed the extreme pleasure we experience in meeting one of our countrymen in a distant region; besides we were brethren of the same order, and had quitted our country for the same **motive.** I was therefore welcome to him on many accounts; nor did he omit any opportunity of convincing me how pleased he was with my visit. He was older **than me,** and had been very successful in his apostolic labours: his house was agreeable and convenient; it was, as I may say, his own work, and the habitation of **virtue.**

His time, which was not employed in the duties of his office, was divided between study and the occupations of the field. He had a
few

few books, the choice of which afforded a good idea of the purity of his morals, and the extent of his knowledge. With the language of the country he was familiar; and the facility with which he spoke it made him very acceptable to many of the Indians, who communicated to him their reflections on all subjects, particularly religion. Affability attracts confidence, and no one was more deserving of the latter than this good man.

He had taught some of the inhabitants of Detroit the French language; and among them I found many whose good sense and sound

judgement

judgement would have made them conspicuous, even in France, had their minds been cultivated by study. Every **day** I remained with this man I found new motives to envy his situation. In a word, he was happy, and had no cause to blush at the means **by** which he became so.

Detroit, or the Narrows, is situated on the strait leading from lake Huron to lake Eri. The country round is said by many to be the finest part of Canada, and seems to want nothing that can make a country delightful: hills, meadows, **fields,** forests, rivulets, fountains, all

all excellent in their kind, and so happily blended as to equal the most romantic wishes. The lands are in general wonderfully fertile, and the islands seem as if placed on purpose to add to the beauty of the prospect. The fort, which is called Pontchartrain*, is on the west side of the strait, and has many Indian villages near it.

* This fort, Niagara, and Michilimakinac, are all situated on the side of the lakes which belong to the United States of America; have ever since the peace been subjects of contention between Great Britain and those states, and by the late treaty of commerce have been delivered up to the Americans.

I re-

I returned from this visit to Niagara, where I remained two years, and in that time learned enough of the Iroquois and Outawah languages to converse in them. This enabled me to enjoy their company when I took a walk in the environs of our post. In the sequel you will see this was extremely useful to me, and saved my life.

When my three years residence at Niagara expired, I was, according to custom, relieved, and passed the winter at the convent at Quebec. It was a great satisfaction to me to pass that rigorous season there. If we we had no superfluities, we however wanted nothing that was necessary; and what was none of our least pleasures, we heard news from our country, and found a society with whom we could converse.

The chaplain of fort Frontiniac fell sick in the spring, and our commissary intended me to supply his place, the situation of which post I have before described. Here I remained two years, when I was recalled to Montreal, and soon after sent to point *La Chevalure*, or Scalping Point, on lake Champlain, so called because the Indians, when they

they kill any one, cut off his scalp, which they carry on a pole, as a proof that they have defeated their enemies. This custom gave a name to the place, as in a battle at this point many Indians were scalped.

Lake Champlain is about fifty-five leagues long; is adorned with several agreeable islands, the waters are good, and well stored with fish. The fort we have at this place is called Frederick, situated advantageously on a very elevated point of land, fifteen leagues from the northern end of the lake, and is the key to the colony of New France,

France, or Canada, towards the English settlements, which are not more than thirty leagues distant.

I did not reach my destination till November, 1735; the season, which began to be severe, increased the fatigues of the voyage, which, except my shipwreck, was one of the most toilsome I have experienced in Canada.

The day we left Chambly, a post about forty leagues from Frederick, we were obliged to sleep out of doors, and during the night there was a fall of snow full a foot deep. The winter came on as it had begun;

gun; and although we found a house at the post to sleep in, our sufferings were almost as great as if we had been in the open air. The house in which we were lodged was not finished; we were but badly covered from the weather, and the walls, which were of an enormous thickness, had been finished but a few days, and added greatly to the inconveniences we received from the rain and snow. Most of our soldiers were afflicted with the scurvy, and we had all such disorders in our eyes, that we were even fearful we should lose our sight. Our food was not better than our lodging. We found little to eat near the post

but

but a few partridges, and to procure venison we were obliged to go as far as lake Sacrement, which was seven or eight leagues off.

In the spring they proceeded to compleat our house, but we chose rather to encamp, during the summer, than to remain any longer therein. **Here we** were not more at our ease, for we were all visited by the fever, and not one of us could enjoy the pleasures of the season. This situation, I must confess, began to be very disagreeable, when towards the month of August I received an order from my provincial to return to France. The
religious

religious who was sent to succeed me was of our province; he arrived at Frederic the 21st of September, 1736, and I departed the same day in the evening. The next day we had a favourable wind, which carried us to point *Au Fer*, about eight leagues from Chambly; but on the 23d we expected to have perished in going down the rapid of St. Teresa: this was the last danger I encountered before I arrived at Quebec, **where** I expected immediately to embark for France.

Thus you have an abridgment of my peregrinations in the new world. Those who have travelled in this

country

country will see I am acquainted with it. The relations of former travellers will inform you of many circumstances which I might have repeated after them; but, in writing my travels, my principal intent was to describe the shipwreck I experienced in my return to France. The circumstances attending it are extremely interesting, and you may prepare to hear a tale of sorrow and woe. All I have to relate will excite your curiosity, and demand your pity; do not be ashamed to bestow it: a good heart is always susceptible of the misfortunes of others. He who does not feel for the misfortunes of his brethren, ought with
justice

justice to be deprived of the happiness of human society.

I remained some time at Quebec waiting an opportunity to return to France; in about two months I found one by the king's ship the Hero, of which I unfortunately did not proffer, but accepted of the offer from the Sieur Frenouse, a Canadian. The connexion between us caused me to accept the place of his chaplain. He was a brave man, whom an experience of forty-six years had rendered very able as a navigator; nor could Messrs. Pacond of Rochelle, the owners, have entrusted their ship, the Renown, in

better

better hands. The vessel was new, a good sailer, very convenient, of about three hundred tons, and mounted with forty pieces of cannon.

Many gentlemen were desirous of going with us, to enjoy a safe and convenient passage, so that we had fifty-four persons on board the vessel. We sailed the 3d of November, with several other ships, and anchored all together in Saint Patrick's Hole, three leagues from Quebec; the next day we reached the island of Orleans. We endeavoured on the 5th to pass the straits of Orleans, but could not, but were more succefsful on the day after, for we paſſed in company with a brigantine bound to Martinico.— The ſhips which ſailed with us had ſucceeded in their firſt attempt; we were therefore without any conſort, and anchored at La Prairie, near the iſle of Coudres.

The 7th we reached Hare Iſland and Mathan, where we found a light wind from the north, the baneful effects of which, and particularly in that ſeaſon of the year, our captain well knew, and confeſſed to us that we had every thing to fear: he thought proper therefore to bear away in ſearch of anchoring ground,

and

and some shelter from the tempest with which we were threatened. A short time after we were obliged to wear, and on the 11th of the month, about eight at night, the wind shifted about to the NNW. NE. ENE. E. at last to the SSE. from whence it blew two days. All this time we were **beat-**ing off the island of Anticosti with reefs in our topsails; but as soon as the wind shifted to the SSE. we steered SE. by E. till the 14th in the morning, when the ship struck, **wi**thin a quarter of a league of the shore, **on** a ridge of rocks, about eight leagues from the southern point of Anticosti.

The ship struck so often, that we were fearful every moment she would go to pieces. The weather may be supposed very bad at this season, and our seamen in despair, since none of them could be persuaded to assist in taking in the sails, although their action on the ship would infallibly hasten our destruction. The water poured into the vessel in great abundance; fear had deprived above half our men of their presence of mind; and a general disorder seemed to announce our approaching dissolution.

If it had not been for our gunner, our future situation would have been dreadful.

dreadful. He ran to the breadroom, and although the water had already made its way in, he threw a quantity of bread between decks. He thought also that some muskets, a barrel of powder, and a case of cartridges, would be useful to us in case we should escape this danger; he therefore caused all these things to be brought up. His precautions were not useless, and without the assistance of these articles I should never have been preserved to relate this. The wind did not abate, nor the sea diminish; the waves carried away our rudder, and we were obliged to cut away our mizenmast. We then began to get our yawl

yawl (the smallest boat of a merchant ship) into the sea, taking great precaution to keep her at a distance from the side of the ship, for fear she should be stove. The sight of death, and hopes of avoiding it, inspired us with courage; and although we knew we must pass a wretched life, at least for many months, in this island, we thought we should be content to suffer every thing, could we pre**serve** our lives.

After having put our yawl into the water, we got our long-boat into the tackles, in order to embark what we could save, and get clear of of the ship quickly, for fear the sea should beat her against the side of the ship, and destroy her. But 'tis in vain for man to rest on his own prudence when the hand of God lays heavy on him. All our efforts were useless. Twenty of us entered the long-boat, and instantly the fore-tackle gave way. Judge of our situation! the long-boat remained suspended by the after-tackle, and of those who were in her many persons fell into the sea, others held by the boat's sides, and some, by means of ropes which hung from the ship's side, got on board her again.

The captain, seeing this accident, ordered the other tackle to be cut or loosened; and the long-boat having regained her position, I jumped into her again to save Messrs. Leveque and Dufresnois, who were nearly drowned. The sea treated our boat so roughly, that the water came in on all sides. Without rudder or sail, in a dreadful storm, a continual rain, the sea raging, and the tide ebbing, what could we look for but approaching destruction! We exerted, however, our efforts to gain an offing; some employed themselves in throwing out the water; we used an oar instead of a rudder: we were in want of of every thing, or every thing went contrary to our intention. Two waves broke over us, and filled the boat with water to our knees; a third would infallibly have sent us to the bottom. Our strength diminished in proportion as we stood more in need of it, and we advanced but slowly, fearing, with great reason, that our boat would founder before we could reach the land. The rain prevented us from distinguishing the place proper for landing; every part we could see appeared very steep, and we beheld nothing before us but death.

I thought it my duty to exhort my companions to put themselves, by an act of contrition, in a proper state to appear before their God. Hitherto I had deferred it for fear of increasing their fears, or abating their courage; but now there was no time to delay, and I did not wish to have to reproach myself with neglect of my duty. Every one betook himself to prayers; and, after the *confiteor* (or confession), I gave them absolution. It was an affecting sight to behold the men labouring to throw out the water, or at the oar; at the same time supplicating God to have pity on them,

and

and to pardon thofe fins which might render them unworthy to participate his glory: they seemed at laft refigned to death, and waited their fate without a murmur. For my part, I recommended my foul to God, and recited the *miferere* aloud, which they all repeated after me. I faw no longer any hope; the boat was ready to founder; and I had covered my eyes with my gown to avoid feeing the moment of my deftruction, when a guft of wind drove us violently on fhore.

You cannot imagine with what hafte we quitted the boat, but we were not immediately out of danger;

the waves rolled over us, some were struck down by them, and we were all in danger of being carried away; we, however, happily resisted their violence, and got off with swallowing much water.

In this scene of disorder, **some one had the** presence of mind to seize the headfast of the boat, and keep her from running adrift, without which precaution we had infallibly perished.

Our first care was to return thanks to God for our deliverance from such imminent danger; and indeed, without his providential aid, it was not possible we should have escaped death. We were now on a sandy point, separated from the body of the island by a river, which ran from a bay a little above where we landed. It was with the greatest difficulty we crossed this river, the depth of which exposed us to danger a third time. As the water ebbed, we were able to fetch what we had in the boat, and bring the articles on shore in the island. This was a great fatigue, but we had no time to lose. We were drenched to the skin, and every thing belonging to us was in the same condition—how then could we possibly make a fire? After a considerable time,

time, however, we succeded: this was more necessary to us than any thing else; and although it was long since we had taken any nourishment, and that we were hungry, we did not think of satisfying that want until we had warmed ourselves.

About three o'clock in the morning the yawl came on shore with only six men in her; the sea ran so high that they could not venture any more. We **went** down to her assistance, and took the necessary precautions to draw her on shore without damaging her. She was our only resource, and without her we
should

should never have been able to get the provisions which the gunner had saved from the ship, nor the seventeen men who still remained on board.

None of us dared to venture the next day, and we passed the succeeding night very sorrowfully. The fire we had made was insufficient to dry us, and we had nothing to serve as a covering in this rigorous season. The wind appeared to increase, and although the ship was strong, new, and well-built, we had reason to fear that she would not remain whole until next day, and that those who were on
board

board would infallibly perish.— About midnight the wind fell, the sea became more calm, and at break of day we saw the ship in the same state we had left her. Some of our seamen went aboard in the boat, and found our men in good health, and that they had passed their time much more agreeably than we had, as they had something to eat and drink, and were under shelter. They put some provisions into the boat, and brought them to us, at a time when hunger began to press us very much.

We then took our repast, consisting of about three ounces of

meat

meat each, a little broth of some legumes or pulse boiled therein. We found it necessary to be careful, that we might not expose ourselves to a total want of food. We sent a second time to the ship to save the carpenter's tools, some pitch for our long-boat, a hatchet to cut wood, and some sails to make tents. All these things were of great use to us, particularly the sails, for the snow fell that night two feet deep.

On the next day, (November 16), while some went on board the ship in search of provisions, others laboured to get the long-boat on shore, and succeeded by help of a double

double tackle. The bad condition she was in convinced us how near we had been perishing, and we could not conceive how it was possible she could have reached the shore. We immediately set about repairing her. The mizen-yard of the ship served for a keel. We made a new stern-post with a piece of timber we cut in the forest; the two planks we wanted for the bottom we got from the ship, and in truth we repaired her as well as it was possible in our situation.

While we were thus employed on our boat we made but one meal in twenty-four hours, and that as moderate

moderate as I have before described. Prudence required this of us; we had only two months provisions in the ship, which is the usual quantity they lay in for a voyage from Quebec to France. All our biscuit was spoiled; and of our other stores, one half had been either consumed or spoiled in the eleven days we had been at sea: so that we had not more than five weeks provisions. This calculation, or, if you please, this reflection, was a melancholy one, for there was no appearance we should be able to quit this desert spot in that period.

The

The ships which pass in the neighbourhood of this island keep too far **off to see any** signals that we **might** have made; besides, the season was so far advanced that we could not expect any until next spring.

I really began to despair; my spirits failed; cold, snow, frost and illness, seemed to unite to increase **our sufferings; and** we were sinking **under the pressure of** so many evils. Our ship became inaccessible by the ice which formed round her; the cold caused a perpetual inclination to sleep, and our tents were insufficient

ficient to protect us from the immense quantity of snow, which fell this year to the height of six feet: many of our companions were already attacked by a fever: such unhappy circumstances obliged us to think of extricating ourselves from them.

We knew that at Mingan, a post situated on the northern shore of the river, or the land of the Eskimaux, there were always some Frenchmen wintered to kill sea wolves for oil. From them we were sure of procuring succour; but the difficulty was, how we should reach that place in such a season; all the small rivers

rivers were already frozen; the snow already covered the earth to the height of three feet, and was daily increasing: the voyage was long, considering the season of the year and our situation, for we **had forty leagues to run to** double the north-west point of the island, afterwards to descend the river St. Lawrence a little way, and then twelve leagues **to run across** the northern **branch of that river.**

We resolved, however, at least to attempt to surmount these obstacles, for in our present situation we could not meet with any thing more dreadful: but a reflection made us

pause

pause for a time. It was not possible that we could all embark at once for Mingan; half the company must necessarily remain here, and those who went would think themselves happy far above the rest, notwithstanding the danger to which they exposed themselves.

We had, however, no other choice to make, and we must either resolve to stay here and perish together in less than six weeks, or to separate ourselves for a time. I informed every one that the least delay would infallibly defeat our plan; that, while we were hesitating, the badness of the weather increased, and

and that we had but a very small stock of provisions. I added, that undoubtedly every individual would be unwilling to remain where we were; but at the same time I represented our separation as absolutely necessary, and I hoped that the Lord would dispose the hearts of some of them to let their brethren depart in search of food: lastly, I entreated them to dry and prepare the ornaments of the chapel; and that, to draw on us the blessing of the Holy Ghost, I would celebrate mass on the 26th; and that I was confident our prayers would procure us the effect we wished. Every one applauded my proposition, and I said

said mass accordingly; at which time twenty-four men offered voluntarily to remain, on condition that those who went would swear on the Evangelists to send succour as soon as they arrived at Mingan.

I informed my companions that I was ready to remain with these twenty-four, and that I would endeavour to encourage them to wait patiently the promised relief.— Every body strenuously opposed my design; and, in order to dissuade me, said, that as I was acquainted with the language of the country, I must accompany those who went in the boats, that in case Messrs.

de

de Frenouse and Senneville, who also spoke the language, should die or fall sick, I might serve as an interpreter to any Indians they might find. Those who were to remain particularly pressed me to go, **as they knew I was incapable of** breaking my word, and did not doubt but that, on my arrival at Mingan, my first care would be to send them assistance. Not but that those who were to go, were very well disposed to send back the boat as soon as possible, but they evidently thought that they might place more confidence in the faith of a priest than **any** other individual.

When

When every thing was arranged, I exhorted those who were to be left at the place of shipwreck to have patience. I told them that the surest means to draw on them the favours of heaven, was to avoid giving themselves up to despair, and to put their trust wholly in Providence; that they should employ themselves in some constant exercise to avoid sickness, and being too much discouraged; that they should use the provisions we left with them prudently, although I hoped to be able to send them relief before they wanted, but that it was better to have some left, than to risk a famine. After I had given them this advice,

advice, those who were to depart began to prepare what they wanted; and on the 27th we embraced our companions, who wished us a happy voyage. On our side we expressed our desire to be able soon to extricate them from their difficulties. We were far from thinking this would be the last time we should see them. Our parting was extremely affecting; and the tears which attended it seemed a kind of foreboding of what was to happen.

Thirteen embarked in the yawl, and twenty-seven in the long-boat: we departed in the afternoon, and rowed about three leagues, but could

not

not find any landing-place, consequently were obliged to pass the night at sea, where we experienced a cold which is not to be described.

The next day we did not make so much way, but we slept on shore; and during part of the night a vast quantity of snow fell on our bodies. The 29th we still had contrary winds, and were obliged by the snow, which continued to fall in abundance, to go on shore early. The 30th the bad weather obliged us to stop at nine o'clock in the morning; we landed and made a good fire, and dressed some peas,

by

by which many of our people were much incommoded.

The 1st of December the wind prevented our embarking, and as our seamen complained of weakness, and said they could no longer labour at the oar, we dressed and ate a little meat, after having also drank the broth: this was the first time since our departure we had fared so well; on the other days we had subsisted on dry and raw salt fish, or else some paste made of meal and water. The second day in the morning, the wind having shifted to the south-east, we sailed, and made good way; about noon we joined the yawl, and had our meal all together. Our joy was extreme to find that the good weather continued, and that the wind was more favourable; but this joy was of short duration, and gave place to a dreadful consternation. After our meal we proceeded on our voyage; the yawl went faster than the long-boat with the oars, but we sailed better than she did. Towards the evening the wind rose and had shifted a little; we therefore thought we should endeavour to double a point we had in sight, and made a signal to the yawl to follow us; but she was too close to the land, and we lost sight of her.

At the point we met with a dreadful sea, and although the wind was not very high, we could not double it but with great difficulty, and after having shipped abundance of water; this alarmed us for the yawl, which was close to the land, where the sea always breaks more than at a distance; in short, she was so severely handled, that she perished—a circumstance, as you will hear, we did not know till the next spring. As soon as we had passed the point we endeavoured to land, but the night was too far advanced, and we could not at first find a place; the sea was for near two leagues full of sharp and high rocks,

rocks, but at laſt ſeeing a ſandy bay, we filled all our ſails, and landed ſafely without being very wet. We immediately lighted a great fire, in order to direct the yawl where we were; but this precaution was uſeleſs, as ſhe was then wrecked.

Having eaten a little of our paſte, every one wrapped himſelf up in his blanket, and paſſed the night near the fire. About ten o'clock the weather grew bad, and the ſnow continued falling till the next day, which the fire melted, and ſo much incommoded us, that we choſe rather

rather to expose ourselves to the cold than to sleep in the water.

Towards midnight the wind was so violent that our long-boat was driven from her anchors, and ran on shore, but was not bulged. The two men who were in her, being asleep, awakened, and called loudly for assistance. We all ran down; the captain and I employed ourselves in throwing what we could of her lading on shore, which the others took up and carried as far as they thought necessary out of the flux of the sea; but the sea became so violent, that in its ebb it would
infallibly

infallibly have carried away the whole, if our companions had not removed them three different times. This was not sufficient; we were obliged to haul up our vessel, and prevent her also from being carried away. The trouble we had to get her on shore is inconceivable, which we did not effect till near ten o'clock the next morning. We found she had suffered greatly, and would require considerable repairs. This we postponed till the morrow, and proceeded to make fires to dry our cloaths; afterwards we ate a small quantity, to restore us after the fatigues we had experienced during the whole night. In the morning the carpenters, and such as were in a condition to assist, worked to replace every thing in a proper state; and a party of our people were employed in searching after the yawl, but without success, and it was in vain for us to continue several days in such a place as this to look for her. On the day before we departed we killed two foxes, which enabled us to save our provisions. In our situation we were glad to avail ourselves of any thing, and the dread of perishing with hunger induced us not to omit any circumstance that would tend to prolong life.

On the 7th of the month at daybreak we failed with a light and favourable wind, which enabled us to make good way. About ten o'clock we ate our foxes, and a few hours after the fky overcaft, and the wind increafing as the tide rofe, we found it neceffary to fearch for a harbour, but could not find any; we were therefore obliged to keep out to fea, and carry a prefs of fail. As the night advanced, a ftorm of rain mingled with hail came on fuddenly, attended with darknefs, and the wind raged fo violently that we could with difficulty fteer the boat, which had already received too many ftrokes to be in a condition

dition for such weather. We were, however, obliged to take our chance.

In the midst of this danger we were driven into a bay, where the wind still tormented us, and we could not possibly finding a landing-place. Our anchor would not bring us up; the weather grew worse every minute, and our boat being driven violently against some sunken rocks, we began to fear our last hour was come.

We exerted all our endeavours, and threw a part of the boat's lading into the sea, to retard our destruction

tion for a short period. This was scarcely accomplished before we found ourselves surrounded with ice; a circumstance which increased our alarms, as the pieces of ice were furiously agitated, and some of them struck against the boat. I am not able to tell you how or where we were driven, but I do assure you the circumstances which agitated us during this night are not to be expressed; darkness augmented the horror of our situation; every stroke of the sea seemed to announce approaching death. I exhorted every one not to despair of Providence; at the same time to prepare themselves to appear and render an account

count before God of a life which had been granted to us only to serve him, who was the master, and entitled to take it away when he pleased.

At last the day appeared, and we endeavoured to get between the rocks and the shore, where, when we succeeded, we found ourselves a little more at our ease. Every one of us conceived ourselves escaped from the jaws of death, and returned thanks to that All-powerful Hand that had preserved us from such imminent danger.

With every effort we could make we could not come near the shore, the

the water was too shallow for the boats; we therefore were forced to cast anchor, and in order to get on shore were obliged to wade through the water, in some places as high as our waists, and every where as high as the knees. We carried on shore our kettle, and some meal to dress. After having taken some nourishment we dried our cloaths, with intent to depart next day.

The cold increased so much during the night that the bay was frozen over, and our boat fast on all sides; we vainly hoped that some gust of wind would break the ice away, for the cold increased every day.

day. The ice continued to grow stronger, and we had no other course to take but to land the few things which had not been thrown into the sea, and to get our provisions round us. We proceeded to make cabins or huts, and covered them with branches of the pine tree. The captain and I were pretty well acquainted with the method of building these huts, and therefore ours was the most convenient. The seamen built one for themselves near us, and we constructed a place to stow our provisions, into which no one could enter but in presence of all the others. This was a ne-cessary precaution, and to prevent such

such suspicions as might have attached to those who had the care of them, and to prevent any one consuming in a few days what ought to support so many persons for a long period.

The furniture of our apartments consisted of an iron pot, in which they formerly used to heat pitch, but now served us for a kettle; we had only one hatchet, and were even in want of a stone to sharpen it: to preserve us against this severe cold we had only our common cloaths and blankets half burned. Any one of these failing, our destruction was inevitable. Without the

the pot it was not poſſible to dreſs any thing to ſupport us; without the hatchet we could not procure any wood to make our fire; and if deprived of our blankets, bad as they were, there was no poſſibility of ſupporting the exceſſive cold of the nights.

This ſtate, you will ſay, was very dreadful, and could not poſſibly be worſe. Here you muſt excuſe me; for although it may appear incredible to you, yet our diſtreſs was really conſtantly augmenting, and I have many things to relate before I ſhall have deſcribed the miſery to which we were reduced.

Our

Our only resource was prolonging our lives till the end of the month of April, and to wait until the ice was dispersed, or melted, that we might be enabled to compleat our voyage in our boat. The chance of any succour reaching us in this place was so little, that we could not even flatter ourselves with any such hope. In this conjuncture it became necessary to examine carefully the state of our provisions, and to regulate the distribution in such a manner that they might last the necessary time. We therefore settled our allowance in the following manner:—in the morning we boiled two pounds of meal in melted snow,

snow, to make either a pudding or porridge: in the evening we dressed about an equal quantity of meat in the same manner. As we were seventeen, each person was consequently allowed about four ounces of nourishment a day. We had no bread, or any other eatable except a few peas, which we boiled once a week instead of meat; and although we had only about a spoonful each, this was in truth our best meal. Fixing the quantity of food we were to be allowed was not enough, it was also necessary to regulate our employment. Myself, Leger, and Basil, undertook to cut all the wood that should be wanted, let the weather

ther be good or bad: others undertook to carry it home, and others to make paths in the snow in the **way we must go** into the forest.

You will perhaps be **surprised** that I should undertake to cut wood, as an employment not proper for me, and **to which my strength was** inadequate. In one respect you are right, but if you reflect that violent exertions open the pores, and give a vent to many humours which would be dangerous **if they remained in** the blood, you will perhaps conclude with me, that to this exercise I am indebted for my preservation. I always took care to labour till I

was

was fatigued, when I felt myself heavy or inclined to a fever, and particularly when I found myself affected by any bad air. We therefore went every day into the woods, and notwithstanding the efforts of our friends to clear away the snow, we often sunk up to the waist in it. This was not the only inconvenience we experienced in this business; the trees within our reach were full of branches, and so covered with snow, that on the first stroke of the hatchet, the man who gave the stroke was knocked down by what fell on him. We all in our turns experienced this treatment, and sometimes we have been
served

served so two or three times successively; we, however, continued our work, and when by repeated strokes we had cleared the tree of spars, we cut it down, chopped it in pieces, and every one returned to the hut loaded: then our companions went in search of the rest which we had cut, or for as much as we wanted for the day. We found this business very fatiguing, but it was absolutely necessary; and although our exertions were extreme, we had every thing to fear if we relaxed in our assiduity: the labour was also daily increasing, for as we cut down the trees, we were obliged to go further in search of others, and consequently

sequently to clear a longer path: unhappily also our strength decayed as our labour increased. Some branches of pine trees, thrown down without order, served us for beds; the vermin tormented us, for we had no change of linen; the smoke and snow caused us inconceivable pains in our eyes, and, to complete our misfortunes, we were troubled with a costiveness, and at the same time an almost continued *diabetes*. I must leave to physicians the task of examining how those two inconveniences could arise. Had we known the cause, it would have been of no service to us; and it is useless to discover the source of an evil

when

when we have no remedy in our power.

The 24th of December we dried the ornaments of our chapel, and as we had still a little wine, I caused it to be thawed, and on Christmas-day celebrated mass. At the conclusion I pronounced a short discourse, to exhort my flock to patience. I drew a parallel between the sufferings of the Saviour of the World and their own, and concluded by recommending them to offer up their prayers to the Lord, assuring them that such offerings would give them a title to a recompense. The evils we feel are much

better

better explained than those we see others suffer. **My** discourse had the effect **I** expected; every one resumed courage, and resigned themselves patiently to suffer what should please God to inflict, either to call us to himself, or relieve us from danger.

On the 1st of January a heavy rain fell all day; and as we **could** not secure ourselves from it, we were obliged to sleep in the wet, and a severe northerly wind blowing in the night, froze us up in our cabin, but broke the ice in the bay, and drove it to sea with our long-boat. A man of the name of Foucault informed

informed us of this dreadful news by a loud cry; and when we had fought every where to find her without effect, you may judge of our consternation. This accident was the severest of our sufferings, and deprived us of every hope of seeing an end to them. I was sensible of its consequences, and beheld every one giving way to despair. Some proposed that we should eat up all our provisions at once, and then quietly lay ourselves down and die: others refused to work; and, to justify their refusal, said, that it was needless to prolong their troubles, since, to all appearance, they could not avoid death. What a situation!

the hardest hard heart must surely be affected with it; the tears flow while I relate it, and you, my brother, are too much awake to the misfortunes of others to suppose that mine will not melt you.

I found it necessary to exert all my abilities to combat the resolutions of my companions; the best reasons I urged seemed to make them more impatient, and to feel with greater poignancy their melancholy situation. That mildness, with which I hoped to be able to turn them from their intentions, not appearing to produce any effect, I assumed that authority my function

gave

gave me, and told them with an energy that seemed to surprise them, "that the Almighty assuredly was "incensed against us, and that he "measured the evils with which he "afflicted us according to the crimes "of which we had been formerly "guilty; that these evil deeds had "undoubtedly been enormous, since "the punishment thereof had been "so severe; but that our despair "was our greatest sin, and that "if we did not soon repent thereof, "would not be pardoned. How "do you know, my brethren," said I, "if you are not near the end "of your repentance? The time of "the most severe sufferings is often

"that

"that of the greatest mercies: do
"not therefore render yourselves un-
"worthy thereof by your mur-
"murs. The first duty of a Chris-
"tian is implicitly to submit to the
"decree of his Creator, and your
"rebel hearts resist him: you lose
"in one instant the fruit of those
"ills which God sends only to
"render those he destines to be his
"children more worthy of his fa-
"vours: you now meditate self-
"murder, and, to avoid some tem-
"porary sufferings, you do not fear
"risking eternal torments. Pur-
"sue, therefore, your criminal in-
"tentions; accomplish your horrid
"designs; I have done my duty,
"and

"and you must determine whether
"you will be lost for ever! I
"hope, however," added I, "there
"are among you some souls so at-
"tached to the law of their God,
"as to respect my remonstrances,
"and that they will join with me
"in offering him their labours, and
"will ask of him strength to sup-
"port him through them."

When I had finished, I was re-
tiring, but they all stopped me, and
entreated me to pardon the state of
despair into which they had fallen,
and, shedding a torrent of tears, assured me that they would no longer
offend Heaven by their murmurs
and

and impatience, but would redouble their efforts to preserve a life which they held of God alone, and of which they were not masters. Instantly every one resumed his ordinary occupation; I and my two companions repaired to the woods, and when we returned, the others went out to bring home what we had cut. When they were all assembled, I told them, that, as I had wine for three or four masses, I would celebrate one to request of the Holy Spirit that strength of which we stood in need; and as the 5th of January was a fine day, I performed the ceremony of the mass thereon. I had scarcely finished, when

when M. Vaillant and the ship's steward, named Foucault, a strong and able man, informed us of a resolution they had taken to go in search of the long-boat. I praised their zeal in exposing themselves thus for the safety of their companions. Praise is welcome in any state of life, and self-love never quits us till we die. In less than two hours after these two men had left us, we saw them return with such an air of satisfaction as foretold they had good news to communicate; nor was our conjecture false, for M. Vaillant told us, that after he and Foucault had travelled for about an hour, they perceived, on the side of the wood, a little hut, and two bark canoes; that, on entering the hut, they had found some fat of the sea wolf and a hatchet, which they brought away with them. Impatience to impart this good news to their companions prevented them from further search. I was in the woods when they returned, and the Sieur Senneville ran to inform me of the discovery these gentlemen had made. I hastened my return to the hut, and entreated the two gentlemen to tell me what they had seen, and every word infused hope and joy into my mind. I seized this opportunity to exalt the cares of Providence towards

those

those who do not despair; and I exhorted every one to return thanks to God for the favour now bestowed on us. The nearer we are to danger, the more gratitude we feel to our deliverer. A few days ago we thought ourselves abandoned without resource, and when we despaired of receiving any help, we learned that there were some Indians in the island, and that towards the end of March, when they returned to their huts in search of their canoes, they might assist us.

This discovery renewed the hopes of those who had made it, and they set off the next day full of that confidence

fidence which a beginning of success inspires. They had hopes of finding our long-boat again, and were not disappointed; for having travelled a little further than they did the day before, they saw her at a distance from the land, and in their return found and brought away with them a trunk full of cloaths, which we had thrown into the water the night before the boat was on the rocks.

On the 10th, although the weather was extremely cold, we all went to endeavour to get our long-boat into a place of safety; but we found her full of ice, and the ice

about

about her made her appear like a little mountain—in short, we saw it was impossible to get her to the shore: a hundred men would scarcely have succeeded, and many would have been in danger of perishing in the attempt. This event gave us much uneasiness; but it was probable that the Indians, to whom the canoes belonged, had some other embarkation with which they had come into the island, and of which we hoped to avail ourselves. We were therefore returning to our home, but had scarcely gone fifty paces, when the cold seized M. Foucault, so as to prevent him from walking: we were obliged to carry him to

our

our cabin, where he foon after expired.

On the 23d our carpenter expired from the fatigue he had undergone; he had time to confefs himfelf, and died a true Chriftian. Although many of us were troubled with fwelled legs, we did not lofe any more until the 11th of February. The expectation of fupporting life till the end of March kept up our fpirits, and we already fancied we faw our deliverers approach. But it was not the will of God: his defigns are impenetrable, and although events turn out contrary to our expectation, we cannot, without blafphemy,

phemy, accuse him of injustice. What we call evil, with him is often designed as a blessing; and whether he rewards or punishes, whether he tries us by adversity or prosperity, we equally owe him our thanks.

Our captain, M. de Frenouse, died on the 16th, after receiving extreme unction. A man of the name of John Bosseman followed him in a few hours, confessing himself, and expiring with great resignation. Towards the evening of the same day, a young man named Girard paid the last debt to nature. A disorder in his legs arose from

warming

warming them too near the fire, and made him feel his approaching end. I assisted him in his last moments, and his repentance of his faults makes me hope he has obtained pardon.

Our gunner fell into a swoon the same night, from which he never recovered. Lastly, a man named Robert Bosseman was attacked by the disorder which had carried off the others. He was a Calvinist, and I wished him to abjure his religion, but I confess it was a difficult task to make him a Catholic. Happily the goodness of the cause I fought supplied the place of those talents

talents neceffary to fupport it. I muft confefs that the reformed are well inftructed, and I was twenty times ftaggered by the reafonings of this man. What a pity that the foundation of Calvinifm fhould be laid on a falfe principle—I will explain myfelf clearly, what a pity that the Calvinifts are not of the Roman communion; with what fuccefs would they defend a good caufe, who can fo vigoroufly fupport a bad one.

At laft this man comprehended me; and being defirous of avoiding the danger of dying in any other belief

belief than ours, on the 24th of February he abjured his religion, repeated the profession of faith, and went to receive his reward in the other world. As these men died, we laid them in the snow near our hut. Undoubtedly it was not prudent to deposit our dead so near us, but we wanted both spirits and strength to carry them farther off; besides, our situation did not allow us to attend to every thing, and we had either no apprehensions of the danger arising from the corruption they might cause in the air, or rather, we thought that the excessive coldness of the air would prevent

that

that corruption from producing those effects which were to be feared at another season.

So many deaths in so short a space of time alarmed us all. However unhappy mankind may be, they view with horror that moment which will relieve them from their cares, if it also deprives them of life. Some of our companions regretted the loss of their wives and children, and wept in contemplating the state of misery into which their deaths would plunge their families; others complained of Heaven in depriving them of life at the moment when they began to

enjoy

enjoy it; others, sensible to the charms of friendship, attached to their country, and destined for agreeable and advantageous establishments, poured forth such lamentations as it was not possible to hear without shedding tears: every word they uttered pierced my heart, and I had scarcely strength enough to comfort them; I mingling my tears with theirs, as I could not refuse them that comfort, or condemn them for complaining. The latter would have been dangerous, and it appeared to me better to let the first emotion of their reflections pass away. The objects they regretted did not render them culpable,

pable, and why should I condemn their grief? To impose silence on an occasion in which insensibility would be blameable, would have been to reflect on human nature.

The situation in which we now were could scarcely be rendered more unhappy; to be approaching death ourselves; to see our friends dying, without ability to assist them; to be in doubt respecting the fate of thirteen of our company who were in the yawl when she was wrecked; and to be almost certain that the twenty-four we left on the place of shipwreck were in as unhappy a state as ourselves; to be
badly

badly fed, badly cloathed, fatigued, diseased in our legs, eat up by vermin, and continually blinded either by the snow or smoke—such was our wretched state. Every one of us was an image of death, and we trembled when looking at each other. What passed in my own mind justified the lamentations of my companions. The more violent our grief is, the shorter is its duration, and expression is denied to heavy misfortunes rather than light ones.

As soon as I saw them absorbed in that silence which usually follows the flood of tears occasioned by any misfortune,

misfortune, and which is the sure mark of excessive grief, I endeavoured to comfort them, and addressed them nearly as follows:

"My dear children, I cannot
"condemn your lamentations, and
"God will doubtless hear them fa-
"vourably, for we have often in
"our misfortunes experienced his
"goodness. Our boat preserved
"on the night of our shipwreck,
"the resolution of twenty of our
"companions who have devoted
"themselves for our preservation,
"and the discovery of the two
"Indian canoes, are circumstances
"which evince the protection which
"God

"God has granted to us. He be-
"stows his blessings only by de-
"grees; and, before he wholly re-
"lieves us, expects we should ren-
"der ourselves worthy, by a due
"resignation to the evils he has
"thought proper to inflict. Do
"not despair of his goodness, and
"he will never abandon those who
"submit to his will. If God does
"not instantly release us, he has,
"however, conducted our friends
"to a spot where the canoes assure
"us we shall soon find a deliver-
"ance. By the help of these ca-
"noes, and the approach of the
"month of March, when the In-
"dians return, we may rest assured
"the

" the time of our deliverance will
" not long be delayed."

I then fell on my knees, and recited such prayers as became our situation and wants, in which every one joined, each appearing to forget his misfortunes for a moment. We remained after this pretty quiet until the 5th of March, beholding, with joy, the time of our deliverance draw near: but God was pleased to afflict us still further, and put our patience to further proofs.

The 6th of March being Ash-Wednesday, about two in the morning

ing a heavy fnow, driven by a violent northerly wind, brought our misfortunes to their height. The fnow fell in fuch immenfe quantities as foon to fill our cabin, and oblige us to take fhelter in that belonging to the feamen, into which the fnow came in alfo very faft; but as it was larger, we had more fpace: our fire was put out, and we had no means to light it again; and, to keep ourfelves warm, we had no other refource but to lay all together, and as clofe as we could. We therefore removed into the feamen's cabin in the morning, carrying the remains of a fmall raw ham, part of which we ate as foon as we entered:

entered: we afterwards removed the snow into a corner of the cabin, and extended the large blanket on the ground, under which we all laid ourselves, and the tatters of the small blankets defended us better from the snow than from the cold. We remained in this state, without fire and victuals, or swallowing any thing but snow, until Saturday morning.

I then took a resolution, notwithstanding the cold, to venture out, and to endeavour to get a little wood, and meal to make some paste. Our lives were at stake if we did not seek some succour against cold

cold and hunger. In the three days and nights we had passed in the seamen's cabin, four **or** five of the crew **had died** with their legs and arms entirely frozen, and we were happy in escaping from the like disaster, for the cold was **so** severe on those **days, that the** stoutest man would have been struck dead had he quitted the hut for ten minutes. You may judge from what I am now **going** to relate : **on** Saturday **the weather was** somewhat milder; I determined **to go** out, and Leger, Basile, and Foucault followed me; we were not more than a quarter of an hour employed in getting the meal, and yet Basile and Foucault had

had their hands and feet frozen, and died, as you will see, a few days after.

It was not possible for us to reach the woods, as the snow had rendered them inaccessible, and we must have risked our destruction if we had endeavoured to remove that obstacle; we were therefore obliged to eat our paste cold—each of us had about three ounces, and were in danger of paying for this little relief with our lives; for, during the whole night, we were tormented with such excessive thirst, and felt such burning heats, as made us think

think we were every moment going to be confumed.

Sunday, the 10th, Meffrs. Tuft, Leger, and I, took the opportunity of fome fine weather to go in fearch of fome wood. We were the only perfons who were able to walk; but it was a miracle that the cold we endured, and the fatigue we underwent in removing the fnow, did not reduce us to the fame condition with the others: happily we were enabled to refift both, and we brought home fome wood, made a fire, and with fnow and a little meal we made a clear porridge, which quenched our thirft a little.

All the wood we were able to bring was confumed by eight o'clock in the evening, and the night was fo cold, that in the morning M. Vaillant, the father, was found dead. This accident made fome of us propofe to return to our own cabin, which was fmaller, and confequently warmer than that of the feamen's. No more fnow **fell,** nor was there any appearance that there would be. Notwithftanding our weaknefs, we undertook to clear our old abode from the fnow and ice which filled it, and we brought fome frefh branches of the fir tree to make our bed; we carried in alfo fome wood, and made large fires both within and

and without to warm it on all sides. After these operations, which greatly fatigued us, we went in search of our companions. M. de Senneville and the younger Vaillant had their legs and arms frozen, and we were obliged to carry them. Messrs. Le Vailleur, Basile, and Foucault, who were less afflicted than the others, removed without much help; we laid them on the branches we had prepared, from whence none of them were ever removed till after their deaths.

On the 17th, Basile lost his senses, and died a few days after. Foucault, who was of a strong con-
stitution

stitution and young, suffered violently; the agonies he experienced in struggling with death made us all tremble, and I never beheld such a dreadful spectacle. I endeavoured to acquit myself of my duty on these occasions, and I hope, with the divine blessing, that my cares of the dying were not useless to their salvation.

Our provisions began to be exhausted: we had no more meal, and there remained only about ten pounds of peas; we had only about seven pounds of candles, the same quantity of bacon, and a small ham which did not weigh more than three

three pounds. It became therefore neceſſary to look for ſome other means of ſubſiſtence. Leger and I, for **M. Furſt,** our ſecond captain, was not in a ſtate to go out, went in ſearch of ſhell fiſh at low water; the weather was tolerable, **and** we waded **through** the water for two hours as high as our knees. At laſt, on a ſand bank, we found a ſpecies of oyſter with a plain ſhell, **and** carried as many home as we could; they were good—and every time the weather and tide permitted, we went in ſearch of ſuch kind of food; but we had like to have paid dear for it, for our legs and hands ſwelled, and were nearly frozen.

I was

I was fully sensible of the danger in attending this kind of fishing too often—but what could we do?—we must live, or rather drive away death for a time.

Our sick grew worse every day; the gangrene, or mortification, took place in their legs, and as no one could dress them, I undertook that office. It was my duty to give an example of that charity which is the foundation of our holy religion; I however hesitated some moments between the merit of fulfilling my obligations, and the danger attending them. God assisted me with resolution to triumph over my repugnance,

pugnance, and I did my duty; and although the time in which I was employed in dreſſing their wounds was **to** me the moſt diſtreſſing of **the** whole day, I never ſlackened in that duty towards them. When I explain the nature of their **wounds, you will judge** whether the reluctance I felt at firſt to dreſs them was without reaſon, or rather if it was not excuſable. I was, however, well rewarded for my trouble; the gratitude **of** the poor ſick men was inconceivable. "What," ſaid one, "ſhall you expoſe yourſelf to "death to preſerve our lives?— "leave us to our misfortunes; your "cares may relieve, but they can
"never

" never cure us."—" **Retire,**" said another, " and do not deprive those who are not to die of the consolation of having you with them: **only assist in** putting us into a state **to appear before God, and** render an account of our days; fly therefore the infected air which is around us."

You may naturally suppose that these kind entreaties attached me the more to them; they augment the pleasure **we** feel in doing our duty, and increase our strength and resolution to perform it.

I soon

I soon saw that our sick men must inevitably die, and they were assured of it themselves; and although they **were** reconciled, I did not think myself dispensed from assisting them in their last moments. I prayed with them morning and evening, **and endeavoured to** confirm them in their submission to the will of heaven. " Offer up your sufferings," said I, " to Jesus Christ, and they " **will render** you worthy of the " **fruit of** the blood he has shed " for the human race: he was a " perfect model of that patience " which I admire in you; your " exile is nearly finished: what
" thanks

"thanks do you not owe him to
"have furnished you, by t**his** ship-
"wreck, with the surest means of
"reaching the port of your salva-
"tion. True, my friends, you
"leave **behind you wives and chil-**
"**dren who look up to you for**
"**support**; but trust in God, he is
"a good father, who never abandons
"his children; **and rest assured**
"**that, in calling you to him, he**
"**will not forget that you leave**
"**behind you families who require**
"his **cares."**

The poor dying men could only
answer by assuring me that they
put their whole **trust** in God, and
thought

thought of those they had left behind, only to recommend them to his care and **protection.** When I had finished speaking to them of spiritual things, I attended to the dressing of their wounds. To clean them I had not any thing but urine, **and I covered them with** some pieces of linen which I dried for that purpose; and when I removed these they brought away part of the flesh **with them,** which, from its corrupted **state,** diffused an infectious air even without side the cabin.

In ten or twelve days there remained nothing of their legs but **the** bones; their feet fell off, and their

their hands were **wholly** void of flesh. The infection was so great, that, when I was dressing the wounds, I was obliged to go into **the** open **air** almost every minute to avoid being **suffocated.** God is my witness I do not exaggerate, and that their situation was more dreadful than I am able to describe. **Expression would** fail **me were** I to endeavour to describe the wretched situation in which I then was.

On the 1st of April Leger went towards the place where the Indian canoes were, and I went into the woods about eight o'clock in the morning. I was sitting to rest myself

self on a tree which I had cut down, when I thought I heard a gun fire; but as we had often thought we heard the same noise, and were never able to discover from whence it came, nor what it really was, I did not pay any great attention. About ten I returned to the cabin to ask M. Furst to assist me in bringing home the wood I had cut. I told him what I had heard, and looked at the same time to see if M. Leger was returning. We had gone hardly two hundred paces when I perceived several persons: I ran to meet them, and M. Furst ran back to carry this happy news to our sick. When I was

near

near enough to diftinguifh objects, I faw an Indian and his wife, whom M. Leger was conducting. I fpoke **to the man,** and he afked feveral queftions, which I anfwered. At the fight of our hut **he was much** furprifed, and greatly affected at the ftate to which we were reduced. He promifed us to return the next day, and that he would hunt in the mean time, and bring us the game he fhould kill.

We paffed the night in expectation that he would perform **his** promife, and in returning thanks to God for the fuccour he had fent us. The day appeared, but our hopes
were

were difappointed; the morning paft away, and the Indian did not appear. Some flattered themfelves he would come in the afternoon; for **my** part I fufpected the real caufe of his abfence, and propofed that we fhould **go to his hut,** and afk the reafon why he did not keep his word, and, if he hefitated in his anfwer, compel him to difcover the place **where the veffel was in which he had croffed into the ifland. We** proceeded; **but** judge of our furprife when we came to the fpot! we found neither Indian nor canoe; he went off in the night, and we could not poffibly difcover him.

To

To let you into the reason of such conduct, I must inform you, that Indians fear death and sickness more than any other people, and the flight of **this savage** arose from that fear which is peculiar **to his nation;** the appearance of our sick men, the dreadful state of their disorders, and the **infection of their wounds,** had so much alarmed him, that, **to** avoid any bad consequences, he had broken his word, and changed his place of residence, for fear we should force him **to** return to our cabin and assist us.

Although this disappointment greatly afflicted us, we should have felt

felt it much more if there had not been a second canoe; but it was necessary to take some measures to prevent the persons to whom she belonged from going away with her also. We were fearful that the Indian who **had played us** this trick might inform his companions of the danger there might be in approaching our cabin, and might persuade **him to** remove his canoe **also in** the night, and quit our neighbourhood.

These reflections induced us to take away the canoe, and thereby oblige the savage to come to our **hut and** assist us, however repugnant it it might be to his **feelings**. Without this precaution we must have perished: neither of the opportunities we had to escape would have **availed us, and** our deaths would have been certain. **The canoe we** made fast to a tree, so that it was not possible to carry her away without giving us an alarm.

Some days past in expectation of seeing the Indian to whom the **canoe** belonged, but no one appeared, and **during** that **period of** time our three sick men died.

On the 7th, in the evening, M. Le Vasseur was seized with a fainting,

ing, from which he never recovered; and the two others, seeing that **even the** assistance we expected **from** the Indian would be useless to them, as they were not in a condition to walk, began to prepare themselves for **death**.

The younger Vaillant died on the 10th, after having suffered for a month **beyond** what it **is** possible to imagine, and his patience was equal to his sufferings; he was only sixteen years of age, and son of M. Vaillant who died the 8th of March. He never complained of the hardship of being snatched out of the world at **so early an age**, but expired

expired with that resignation and courage which characterizes a perfect Christian.

M. Senneville imitated the virtues of M. Vaillant, or rather they served as models to each other—the same afflictions, the same patience, the same resignation. I wish I could repeat correctly what those two young men said to me a few days before their deaths; they made me blush to want that courage to comfort them which they had to suffer. With what respect and confidence did they speak of religion and the mercies of God? In what terms did they express their gratitude?

titude? They certainly poffeffed the beft minds and beft hearts of any young **men I ever** knew.

The latter often requefted me to amputate his legs, to prevent the gangrene fpreading. **You may fup-pofe his** requeft was ufelefs, and I conftantly refufed. I reprefented to him that I had no inftruments proper for the operation; **and** that **if I was** to attempt it, far from eafing, it would only augment his pain, without faving his life. He then fettled his affairs, wrote to his parents in the moft affecting manner, and on the 13th refigned his foul at the age of twenty. He was
a Ca-

a Canadian, son of M. Senneville of Montreal.

The death of these three victims to cold and hunger greatly affected me, although their lives may be said to have been burdens to them. I had the affection of a father to them, and they made a suitable return; yet when I reflected that had the Indian returned while they lived, I must have left them alone and destitute in the hut, or have lost the opportunity of getting away, I thought I ought to thank the Lord for having spared me so cruel an alternative, by taking the dying men to himself. Besides, we had

had now none of our provisions left, except a small ham which we were afraid to touch, **and we** contented ourselves **with** such shell **fish as** Leger and I could from time to time pick up on the sea side. Our weakness was daily increasing, **and** we were **scarcely able to su**pport ourselves, when I took the resolution to go in search of the Indians whose arrival we expected, and for that purpose to make use of their **canoe.** To repair it we got some gum from the trees, and with our hatchet made two paddles as well as we could. I knew very well how to paddle, which was a great advantage for the execution of our design,

design, and even might induce us to venture, in case we could not find any Indians, to cross the river in the canoe. This was our last resource; for, when life is at stake, we willingly run every risk. We were sure that we could exist but a few days longer in this island—in venturing to cross we only risked life, and we might succeed.

On the 26th of April all was ready, we dressed our piece of ham, and first ate the broth, with intention to reserve the meat **for our** voyage, but in the evening we were so pressed with hunger, that we were obliged to eat the whole.

H 4   Next

Next day we did not find any increase of our strength, and we were without resource, and no prospect of finding any in time to preserve us from perishing; we prepared ourselves therefore for death, reciting the litany of the Saints; and throwing ourselves on our knees, I pronounced this prayer:

"Great God! if 'tis your will
"that we meet the same fate with
"the forty persons who have pe-
"rished under our eyes, hasten to
"accomplish it; do not permit us
"to despair, but call us from the
"world in this our present state of
"resignation. But, O Lord! if
"our

" our death **is now** decreed, send
" us help, and give us strength
" to support, without complaining,
" those afflictions which thy justice
" has prepared, that we may not
" lose **in an instant the** fruit of that
" submission which we have hitherto
" manifested for the decrees of thy
" providence."

I had scarcely ended my prayer, when we heard the firing of a musket, which we soon answered, and concluded **it** was the Indian to whom the canoe belonged: **he** wanted to know if any of us were alive, and being assured we were by answering his signal, he lighted

his

his fire. He did not suppose we were in a state to go to him, and apparently **did** not wish we should; for, as soon **as** he perceived us, he hid a part of a bear he had killed in the woods, and ran away.

As we were **in** boots **we** found much difficulty in getting to his fire, for we were obliged to cross a pretty large river, and which had been thawed a few days. We fol**lowed** his track, but with incredible fatigue, which would have been useless if the Indian had not been obliged to stop for his child, a boy **of** about seven years of age, to follow him. This circumstance preserved

ferved us. We **overtook** him towards the evening, and **he** directly afked us if our fick men were dead. This queftion, which he afked with **apparent** fear that they were yet alive, **convinced us** that the other Indian had informed him **of our** fituation, and of the rifk he would **run** by coming **near** our abode. I did not think proper to anfwer his queftion immediately, but, without any circumlocution, preffed him to return back, and give us fomething to eat. He dared not refift; we were two to one, well armed, **and** fully refolved not to quit him for a moment. He then confeffed he had a bear almoft whole, which he was

ready

ready to share with us. When we returned to the place where he had hidden the bear, **we each** of us eat a bit half **dressed, and** then we made him and his **wife eat,** and conducted them to the spot where we had left M. Furst. This poor man **waited** for us **with great impatience,** and we found him almost exhausted. Judge how great his joy must be, when we informed him that we had got both provisions and help. He eat at first **a piece of the** bear, and we put the pot on the fire, and kept it there the whole night, taking occasionally some of the broth. We dared not go to sleep, for fear the savage, who would not enter the hut,

hut, should **run away.** As soon as the day appeared, I gave him to understand that he must conduct us **to** the place where the boat lay which had brought him into this **island;** **and to engage him** to do so, I told him we should treat him very ill, if he did not consent speedily. Fear of death set him speedily **to work to make a sleigh,** or sledge, on which he fixed his canoe, and made signs for Loger and me to draw it. Undoubtedly he wished we should fatigue ourselves, and **give up the succour** which would cost us so dear. We might easily have compelled him to drag the canoe himself, but I did **not**

not think that would be proper; as it was neceſſary to humour him, and only take ſuch precautions with him as not to be made his dupes.

I deſired the Indian and his wife to walk before us, under pretence of clearing the way; but I did not confine my precautions to them only; I told them I thought the child would be too much fatigued in walking, and would put him into the canoe, as it would be a pleaſure to us to relieve him.

The heart of a parent is every where the ſame; there is no one **who** does not conceive himſelf under an obligation for the service done to his child, and accepts it with pleasure. Thus the boy became a hostage to us for the fidelity of his father. We walked in this way, for above a league, either in snow, in water, or upon ice; our fatigue was extreme, but hopes of the relief we should find supported and gave us courage. We could not, however, possibly continue to drag this canoe, and were nearly exhausted, when the Indian, touched with our situation, took it on his shoulder, carried it to the sea, and put his wife and child on board. As the canoe could hold only four persons, and consequently there was but one of us

three

three who could embark, the question now was, which should be the man? I offered to stay, and to let Messrs. Furst and Leger agree between themselves which should go. Each of them wished to have the preference, and were **fearful of losing this** opportunity **of avoiding** an unhappy end. While they were disputing, the Indian made signs for me to come forward, and told me he guessed the cause of dispute between my **two** companions, and that he would take none but me. Without giving time for reply, he pulled me into the canoe, and pushed off.

Messrs.

Messrs. Furst and Leger then **deemed** their destruction certain, and loudly expressed their despair. I could not resist, and begged the Indian to draw near the shore, that I **might** speak a **few** words of consolation to my companions. When I was near enough, I justified my conduct towards them by repeating what **the Indian had said,** and advised them to keep along the sea shore; and promised, on the word of a divine, that, as soon as I reached the Indian's hut, I would come back to them with the canoe. They knew me incapable of perjuring myself; the assurances I gave them calmed their minds, and they

saw

saw us put to sea without inquietude.

We landed the same day, and the Indian took his canoe on his shoulders, carried it near the wood, and laid it on the snow. As I was **fatigued with being** so long on my knees in the canoe, I laid myself down to rest on a stone by the sea side; and thinking, after some time, that the Indian was lighting his fire with intent to sleep in that place, I took up my gun, two paddles, and two large pieces of meat, which I had put into the boat to save Messrs. Leger and Furst the trouble of car**rying** them, and climbed up upon
some

some ice which was six feet high at least. I was no sooner there, than I saw my Indian and his wife had put on their rackets, which are a kind of snow shoes which the Canadian **Indians use to** walk quick on the snow. The man took his boy on his shoulders, and both ran as hard as they could: the cries I made **to stop them** only **made them** fly the faster: as soon as I could throw away my paddles, I got down the ice, and with my gun and my meat pursued their track for some time.

In getting up on the ice I wounded my right leg considerably, which

which received additional injury in my running—every step my leg sunk into the snow, and that was every moment; I lost my breath, and was many times obliged to rest on my gun to recover it. While in this posture, I heard the voice of M. Leger. This meeting gave us both great pleasure. I told him what had passed; and he in his turn informed me that M. Furst, overwhelmed with fatigue, was unable to keep up with him, and that he had left him extended on the snow a considerable distance from where we then were.

At

At any other time I should have flown to his assistance; but as it was of the utmost importance to us to overtake our fugitive, and M. Leger was sensible how much we risked by losing time in pursuing him, we immediately ran towards the place where I knew he had fled; but as he had quitted the snow to take the sea side, which was low and sandy, we were detained some time; we, however, continued our course, and, after walking a quarter of an hour, we discovered the Indian's track: he had quitted his rackets, undoubtedly on a supposition that I could not follow him so far. This

circum-

circumstance made us believe we were not far from his dwelling: we redoubled our speed, and when we approached a wood we heard a gun fire; this we did not think proper to answer, concluding that if it was he who had fired, **he** would put on his rackets to enable him to run with greater haste when he knew we were so near.

We continued walking, and a little time after the first gun fired we heard a second: this made us suspect that the Indian designed to light his fire in this place, and rest himself and family, but that he wished

wished first to know if any one was **in** pursuit of him. Our conjecture herein was wrong.

Ten minutes after the second report we heard a **third, and were so** near that we saw the flash; but we did not answer, and continued to advance **in silence.** On our road we found a **boat,** on which they had been at work, and about twenty paces further we saw a large hut. We entered with an air which agreed with our situation, that of suppliants, but an old man **who** spoke French would not permit us to proceed. " Every man," says he, " is **our equal.** Your misfor-
" tunes

" tunes render you worthy, and I
" look upon it as a favour granted
" by heaven to be furnished with
" an opportunity to do good to
" men whom misfortune has pur-
" fued. I only ask of you a re-
" lation of what has passed since
" you have been in this island; I
" shall be happy to condole with
" you on your past misfortunes,
'' and my sensibility will add to
" your consolation."

At the same time he ordered that our meat should be dressed with some peas, and that nothing should be omitted to prove that humanity is as much a virtue among American

rican Indians as more civilised nations. As soon as he had given his instructions, he requested us to satisfy his curiosity. I did so, and endeavoured to omit no one circumstance which had attended our misfortune. After I had ended my tale, I requested the old man to tell me why the two Indians, whom we had seen in the height of our misfortunes, had refused us any help.

"The Indians," says he, "trem-
"ble at the name of sickness, and
"all my reasoning has not been
"able to dispel that fear from those
"you now see in this cabin. Not
"that they are insensible to the
"mis-

"misfortunes of their brethren—
"they would wish to comfort them,
"but the fear of breathing a cor-
"rupted air, checks that emotion
"in their hearts which naturally
"leads them to compassion. They
"fear death, not like other men;
"and I know not if they would
"not be guilty of the greatest
"crimes to avoid it. There," said
he, shewing me an Indian which
stood behind the others, "is the
"man who broke his word with
"you. He returned to us about
"the beginning of the moon, and
"related to us the dreadful situa-
"tion in which he had seen the
"Frenchmen, whom he thought

"were

" were by this time all dead; but
" he would willingly have given
" them affiftance, had not he feared
" the corruption which raged among
" them. There is the other," faid
he, fhewing me the man I had run
after; " he arrived here before you,
" and informed us there were three
" Frenchmen ftill living, who were
" no longer in the jaws of death,
" but who appeared well, and he
" believed we might venture to
" fuccour them without fear of in-
" fectious air. We had deliberated
" a few minutes; afterwards we
" fent an Indian towards the place
" where you were, that he might
" inform you, by firing three guns,

" of

" of the place of our abode. There-
" fore it was the sickness among
" you which alone prevented us
" from assisting you; and perhaps
" we might have come to you not-
" withstanding, had we not been
" told, that any help we could send
" you would be of no service, and
" that we should run a great risk
" in approaching your dwelling,
" which was filled and surrounded
" with an atmosphere infectious
" and dangerous to breathe."

This discourse, from a man who was one of a nation that a false prejudice had taught us to believe were incapable of thinking, and whom

whom we had unjuftly concluded to be deftitute of fentiment and expreffion, furprifed me greatly. Indeed I muft confefs that, to impart fuch an idea of this Indian as I would wifh to give, it would be neceffary to hear him.

When the old man had ended his difcourfe, I endeavoured to exprefs to him the gratitude we felt, and defired him to accept of my mufket, which, in point of goodnefs and ornaments, was far preferable to any in the hut. I afterwards told him, that fatigue had prevented one of our comrades from following us, and that we fhould efteem it the higheft highest favour if he would send out two of his men to assist us in bringing him in. My entreaties were ineffectual; the Indians are afraid of going out in the night, and we could not procure any to go to M. Furst's assistance, but they promised to accompany me early in the morning. This refusal made me very unhappy; the old Indian saw my uneasiness, and told me it would be useless to seek for my friend in the night, as he had no musket to give notice where he was, and that we had better stay till the morning. M. Furst was therefore obliged to pass the night on the snow, protected from death by the

hand

hand of God alone, for even in the hut we endured a moſt ſevere cold. The Indians make no fire when they ſleep, and theſe had no blankets, conſequently we paſſed a miſerable night.

On the next day, as we were preparing to go in ſearch of M. Furſt, we ſaw him coming towards us; he had followed our traces, and, to come up with us, he had availed himſelf of the hardneſs of the ſnow which the cold of the night occaſions, and which will then ſupport the weight of thoſe who walk on it. Our firſt care was to warm, then to give him ſome refreshment, and we reciprocally expressed our pleasure at meeting each other again.

The 29th and 30th we remained with the Indians; we observed that the attention we paid to some excited jealousy in the rest, and they all endeavoured to surpass each other in their services to us. We were not in want either of the meat of the bear, or carabou, during those days, and they were sure to give us the most delicate pieces. I do not know whether the duties of hospitality are best fulfilled by the Europeans or the Indians, but I am tempted to believe that the

latter

latter execute them with the better grace.

The 1st of May they launched their boat; we all embarked, and set sail. The **wind failed us** at noon, when about six leagues from the continent. This greatly affected me, for fear I should not be able to assist my companions who remained near the place of shipwreck; and in this fear I requested the old man to let me have two men and a bark canoe to get to the shore: With a view to induce him to grant my request, I promised to send to him, and those who were with him in the boat, some tobacco and brandy, as soon

soon as I should get among the French settlers. Although he was willing to oblige me, yet he had a council before he acceded; and it was not without difficulty that my request was granted. They were fearful that a passage of six leagues was too much for a canoe, and they were unwilling to expose us to danger. We departed, however, and about half after eleven at night we reached the shore and settlement. I went into the first house I saw, which belonged to M. Volant, a native of St. Germain en Léye, my friend, and chief of this post. I could not have fallen into better hands, as he had not only the desire,

but

but ability to serve me. At first he did not recollect me, and indeed I was not in a state to be recollected; but as soon as I told him my name, he loaded me with expressions of friendship, and the pleasure we had in meeting each other was extreme. I at first told him of my engagement with the Indians, and brandy and tobacco were prepared for every one of our deliverers. They did not reach us until ten o'clock in the morning, during which interval I gave M. Volant a detail of our adventures, and forcibly pleaded the cause of the twenty-four men who remained near the wreck. My friend was much affected with their

their situation. He immediately prepared a boat to go in search of them, and also if the thirteen men who were in the yawl were still alive. He sailed, and when he reached the neighbourhood in which our ship was wrecked, fired some muskets, to give information to those who had been left there. He soon saw four men, who threw themselves on their knees, and with folded hands entreated him to save their lives. Their haggard looks, and the sound of their voices, which announced them to be on the brink of the grave, affected M. Volant greatly. He joined them, and gave them some refreshment, but very moderate,

moderate, for fear that **too** large a quantity might caufe their deaths. Notwithftanding this judicious precaution, one of them named **Tenguy,** a **Breton, died after drinking a glafs of brandy.**

Twenty-one of the company were dead; thefe my friend ordered to be interred, and the three who had furvived the fatigues, famine, and the rigour of the feafon, we brought away. **It** was, however, a confiderab**le time before** they were reftored to health; one of them, Fourellot, the boatfwain, had intervals of infanity, and the two others, named Baudet and Bonaw, had their bodies

bodies swelled all over. Good food, and the care taken of them, restored them, if not to perfect health, at least they were so recovered as to depart with us for Quebec.

As he returned, M. Volant perceived on the shore two bodies apparently of drowned men, and some remains of a canoe. He drew nearer to be certain of what he saw, and fired some guns to discover if any one was in the neighbourhood. No one appeared or answered, and I therefore concluded that the thirteen men who were in the canoe died of hunger and cold, for my friend saw, at some distance from the

the sea side, a kind of hut, a proof that they had landed, and, being destitute of help, must have perished miserably.

I need not tell you how much we were affected when we saw the three men arrive who had been left behind; you may naturally suppose our interview was very affecting, and that tears were not spared on either side.

After our first emotions, I enquired how they had been able to exist so long, and in what manner their companions had ended their lives. They told me that some had perished

perished by cold and hunger, and others had been carried off by dreadful ulcers; that their wants had been so great that the survivors had eaten even the shoes of their dead companions, after having first boiled them in melted snow, and afterwards broiled them. That when this resource failed, they had recourse to the leather breeches of the deceased, and that when M. Volant found them they had but one or two pairs remaining.

You may see therefore that the situation of these poor men was as afflicting as our own, and that they suffered perhaps more than we did,

parti-

particularly as they were under the neceffity of eating the cloaths of their deceafed companions.

We remained near fix weeks at Mingan, which we employed only in returning thanks to God, who had preferved us in the midft of fuch imminent danger. M. Leger quitted us to go to Labrador, there to get a paffage for Old France; but we took our paffage, on the 8th of June, in a fmall veffel for Quebec, and with a favourable wind reached it on the 13th. Every one was aftonifhed at our return, as they thought we had been in France, and were anxious to know

know what had happened to us since our departure, and we satisfied those who were most concerned to know.

Next day we put the three seamen that M. Volant had brought away into the hospital, and M. Furst and I did all we could for the perfect re-establishment of our health. As soon as I was sufficiently recovered, they gave me the little living of Soulange, which I served for about a year, and then received another order to return to France. I embarked therefore as chaplain to the king's ship the Ruby, and sailed the 21st of October,

ber, 1738, and reached Port Lewis, in Bretagne, the 2d of December, to take in provisions, as our stock was nearly expended. Having supplied this want, we sailed for Rochefort, the place of our destination, where my duty detained me until the ship was put out of service.

THE END.

www.ingramcontent.com/pod-product-compliance
Lightning Source LLC
Chambersburg PA
CBHW020828230426
43666CB00007B/1147